Th...
of Exam Cal...

Anita Naik

h
Hodder
Children's
Books

Text copyright 2000 © Anita Naik
Illustration copyright 2000 © Jennifer Graham
Published by Hodder Children's Books 2000

The right of Anita Naik and Jennifer Graham to be identified as the author and illustrator of the Work has been asserted by them in accordance with the Copyright, Designs and Patents Act 1988.

10 9 8 7 6 5

A catalogue record for this book is available from the British Library.

ISBN: 0 340 77938 1

The information in this book has been thoroughly researched and checked for accuracy, and safety advice is given where appropriate. Neither the author nor the publishers can accept any responsibility for any loss, injury or damage incurred as a result of using this book.

Hodder Children's Books
a division of Hodder Headline
338 Euston Road
London NW1 3BH

'If we did all the things we're capable of doing, we would literally astound ourselves.'
THOMAS EDISON (1847-1931)

Simple but true.
Exams are not the most important
things you will ever do in your life
(no matter what other people say).
The fact is, pass or fail, you are more
than a grade on a piece of paper.
Remember that, and you won't be
sucked head first into the hysteria
of exam season.

BELIEVE IN
YOURSELF

*Think you're not smart enough
to achieve good results?*

Studies show that you do not
have to have an incredibly
high IQ to pass exams.
However, you do have to believe in
yourself and your ability to work.

BE REALISTIC

Think you're the only one getting worried?

•

Be realistic . . . unless you're a closet
Einstein, you're not going to sail
through your exams with zero anxiety.
So relax – it's only natural to
feel stressed.

THINK
POSITIVE

Scared you're going to fail and ruin your life?

You're not alone, as 90% of people who take exams feel like this. Erase your fears by listing them and then ripping the list up.

DEFY YOUR
STEREOTYPE

Do you think of yourself as a no-hoper who's never passed an exam in your life?

It's time to defy your stereotype – you can change the record any time you want.

LEARN TO
FOCUS

Feeling confused and don't know where to turn?

•

Write yourself a mission statement saying exactly what you hope to achieve in your life. This will not only help you to focus on your work, but will also show you that pass or fail; life does exist beyond exams.

RELEASE
STRESS

Do you feel very stressed and panicky?

Try screaming out loud – it releases stress in a major way. Clench up your jaw, then open your mouth wide and let that stress come screaming out.

IGNORE
NEGATIVE
THOUGHTS

Do you have little voices in your head
telling you that you cannot pass exams?

Kill off those voices and banish
all excuses.

PLAN
YOUR TIME

Feel as though time is running out?

It is a waste of precious time not to have a revision plan, so draw up a timetable. Don't let it rule you completely however, and update it when necessary.

BE HAPPY

Think you can pass an exam by being serious and grave?

•

This simply isn't true. Remember to have some fun and let your hair down now and then. Laughter will release your body's 'endorphins' (natural painkillers) and make you feel energised.

TAKE

FIVE

*Can't think or concentrate on what
you're reading?*

Take frequent breaks – preferably one
every forty minutes. Get up, walk
about, or call a friend. Do anything to
distract yourself until you feel better.

LOOK
AHEAD

*Are you feeling a bit bogged down and
claustrophobic whilst preparing for
your exams?*

Invest in some positive thinking.
Start by viewing your exams as
opportunities to your life, not threats.

THINK CALM
THOUGHTS

Are you in the midst of a panic frenzy?

Stop what you're doing and think
'calm'. Then visualise a calm
landscape . . . try thinking of your
favourite holiday destination.

PRIORITISE

Would you like to create more order to your workload?

It is human nature to avoid the difficult, so change that by prioritising the more complex tasks, and not leaving them until the end.

USE YOUR
IMAGINATION

Having trouble remembering a certain important fact?

Don't force yourself to puzzle over it for hours. Simply look it up and associate the information with a strong visual image. The more outrageous the image is, the better you'll retain it.

FOOD FOR
THOUGHT

*Need extra help in boosting
your brain's power?*

Eat more garlic (but consider others,
and opt for garlic tablets). Garlic
improves blood flow through the small
blood vessels in the brain.

BRIGHTEN UP
YOUR LIFE

Would you like to try adopting a new age view?

Surrounding yourself by certain colours is believed to aid stress-related problems. Red brings about confidence, yellow clear thinking and violet helps keep you calm.

GLEAN
INFORMATION

Feel as though you need a new method of revising?

Browse through your books and notes and only read the bits that catch your attention. Do this at least three times and see the amount that your brain picks up.

THINK
REALISTICALLY

*Scared that you can't fit all of
your work in?*

Give yourself a start and finish time.
This way you'll have something to
work towards. Planning helps get rid
of fear of the unknown.

HELP FROM
FRIENDS

Need a little help from your friends?

Testing your friends will help all
of you whilst studying. Asking
other people questions will actually
make it easier for you to recall
and retain answers.

MODERATION

*Are you struggling through a vast amount
of notes, books and essays?*

Don't even try to read everything at
once, as this will just send your head
into a spin. Instead, choose wisely
and stick to key texts, and key parts
of those texts.

FRESH AIR,
FRESH MIND

*Do you feel tired and groggy
when revising?*

Keep your window open. Your brain
uses 20–50% of the oxygen you take
in, so in order to keep fatigue at bay,
you need to breathe clean, fresh air.

BREATH
OF LIFE

*Find yourself heading towards a
full-blown panic attack?*

Remember to breathe – when we
panic we forget to breathe properly. If
you feel short of breath at any time,
put your head between your knees and
breathe slowly and deeply three times.

COOL
DOWN

Feel that things are hotting up?

Keep the temperature cool. If your room is too warm, or you have too many layers of clothes on, you will relax too much and may even nod off.

SPREAD

OUT

Did you know that lack of physical space can make you feel boxed in and frustrated?

Give yourself some decent space to study in. According to the 'Feng Shui' principle, a small space means a small mind, open space means open mind.

DRESS FOR
THE OCCASION

Did you know that where you revise and what you wear can have an effect on how efficient your studying is?

·

Don't wear your pyjamas and study in bed, as your brain won't feel as though you are serious about work.

PURE
CONCENTRATION

Think that you can study when a million other things are cluttering up your mind?

It just isn't possible. Try to clear your mind completely to help you focus on the job at hand.

SWEET
DREAMS

Did you know that our brains continue learning even when we're asleep?

Research shows that 75% of our dreams are related to the activities we immerse ourselves in in the twelve hours before sleep. If these hours are filled with a sensible combination of revision and short breaks, your mind will continue to learn as you sleep.

TREAT
YOURSELF

Have you tried rewarding yourself when you get to the end of a task?

Rewarding yourself like this will make your journey through study easier. Try eating your favourite food, watching television or phoning a friend.

LINK UP

Making diagrams can help your revision.

Make links when studying subjects.
Flow charts, mind maps or word and
illustration-related links work well.
Or think of 'nonsense' rhymes to help
trigger your memory.

TALK
IT OVER

Are you really worried about the exams?

Don't bottle your worries up – it will
only make things worse. Instead talk
them over with somebody and
remember that your parents
took exams too.

TIME OUT

Feeling tired and totally stressed?

Take a day off. It will work wonders
for your body and will allow your
brain to absorb and relate facts.

CHILL OUT

Finding that no matter what you do, the worry is just getting too much?

Remind yourself that worry is coupled with fear. To alleviate the worry, look at exactly what you're afraid of and then put your fear into context.

HERBAL HELP

Do you believe in herbal powers?

Go herbal and try some 'Ginkgo'
(120 mg daily) for a few days. It is
known to increase alertness and
blood circulation to the brain.

GINGER
SNAPS

Feeling harassed and strung out?

Try inhaling some ginger essence or
eat some ginger snaps. Ginger is
supposed to help ease mental
confusion and relieve fatigue.

LITTLE
IS MORE

*Confused as to where to begin in
your studies?*

Studies show that concentrating on
key words rather than piles of notes
will help you to retain information
more successfully.

GET
FLEXIBLE

*Does your body ache from too much
slouching over your desk?*

Too much sitting causes a hunched-over
posture that stops blood reaching the brain.
Shrugging and rolling your shoulders will
help loosen up your neck and shoulder
muscles as well as regaining the blood
supply balance to your brain.

OUT
AND ABOUT

*Did you know that a healthy body equals
a healthy mind and attitude?*

Go outside and get some exercise.
Even a short walk around the block
will help clear your mind.

POWER
POTIONS

*Want to put your trust in
some herbal remedies?*

Invest in some Clary Sage or
Ylang Ylang oil. Rub on your skin
with a base oil to help lose your
anxiety and stress-related fears.

NEAT
NOTES

Would you like to try a new revision method that helps jog your memory?

Write key words on post-it notes and stick them in places you come across throughout the day. Attach them to the fridge, the kettle, the mirror or the television.

MAXIMISE
YOUR BRAIN

Think that your brain needs a workout?

Studies show that the more you exercise your brain in the morning, the better your memory will be all day. This means that you should tackle the more difficult subjects first thing.

STRESS
RELIEF

Agitated with stress and worry?

Try pressing your acupressure points
(an ancient Chinese therapy). Find the
tender place between your thumb and
index finger, apply pressure and release.
Do this three times.

MOTIVATION

Find yourself losing enthusiasm?

It's hard to stay motivated, especially
when you're halfway through exams.
Enthuse yourself with the thought that
in a month's time it will all be over.

ENTHUSIASM

Did you know that thinking positively can really help your chances of passing?

It sounds hard, but being enthusiastic about passing is infectious and the more you encourage others to see that they can pass, the more positive you will feel.

NEVER
TOO LATE

*Feel that you've left it too late
to start revising?*

❋

It's never too late to study for an exam
or ask for help.

BE CONFIDENT

Are you lacking in confidence and really fear these exams?

Police your thoughts – don't let the cynical, negative monster inside you eat away all your self-confidence.

DON'T BE SHY

Do you need reminding of just how capable you really are?

Write a list of five positive points about yourself and pin them above your desk. These will remind you that you are not a failure just because you cannot get to grips with a particular subject.

DON'T
GIVE UP

Feel that all is lost just because one exam paper didn't go too well?

It isn't the end of the world if you feel one paper didn't go very well.
Up your recovery rate – carry on thinking positively and start planning for the next.

THINK HAPPY
THOUGHTS

Do you find that negative thoughts are overwhelming you?

Swap irrational thoughts for happy ones.
Instead of thinking of ten reasons why
you might fail, think of ten reasons why
you will pass. Positive thoughts will
inhibit negative feelings and foster an
increase in available energy.

WATCH
YOUR DIET

*Could what you're eating be affecting your
chances of success?*

Change your diet if you think it's
necessary. Carbohydrates and fat make
you tired by mid-afternoon. Instead,
eat more fish because it contains
phosphatidylcholine which is
excellent for the memory.

THE
RIGHT
FOODS

Riveted with boredom fatigue?

Eat more foods with B vitamins, such
as cheese, beef, milk and cereals.
These help improve your memory,
concentration and energy levels.

PACE YOURSELF

Are you feeling tired and fed up?

Remember to eat little and often to keep your blood sugar levels up and at an even level.

STRESS
BALM

Would you like nature to help alleviate your worries?

•

Lemon balm is known as the 'scholar's herb' as it was traditionally taken by students suffering from stress. Herbalists suggest taking 650 mg, three times a day.

MOOD LIFTER

Feel as though you need a mood lifter?

Choose some music that really fires
you up, gets your energy levels moving
and makes you feel uplifted. Play it
loud every time you get despondent.

BREAKFAST
BOOSTER

Feel your energy levels starting to flag by mid-morning?

Never skip breakfast – it is the most important meal of the day. Studies have proved that breakfast helps boost your energy, which is just what you need to keep your brain moving.

SPEAK
TO OTHERS

Feel as though you need extra support?

Seek out your family or friends for
help – whether you want advice,
reassurance, or a shoulder to cry on.

FORGET
PAST EXAMS

Do discussions about previous exams cause you concern?

Don't dissect past exams – you've taken them, they're over, so don't torture yourself with a group discussion.

RECHARGE

*Feel absolutely fed up with
studying all day?*

·

It's important to recharge your
batteries by doing something once a
day that has nothing to do with your
exams. Try taking a long bath, going
for a run or watching a video.

LAST GLANCE

Some time to fill just before the exam?

•

Choose a textbook from the exam's
subject area and open it at any page.
Read just one paragraph and then shut
the book. This will help focus your
mind on the subject.

PRECIOUS
MOMENTS

*Wish that you'd started
revising earlier?*

It is possible to retain some
information with last-minute
cramming. Don't believe those who
say it's too late. It's never too late to
learn something.

THINK OF
YOURSELF

Lacking motivation?

Decide you want to pass the exams for yourself. Not for your mum, your dad, or your teachers. Doing it for yourself will make you feel more energised about studying.

YOU'RE NOT ALONE

Is the whole exam worry dragging you down?

Don't let them. They are just aptitude tests and can always be retaken, which isn't the end of the world. If you really feel as though you cannot cope, tell somebody – a teacher, a parent or a friend. Do not suffer in silence.

Always remember . . .

YOU ARE MORE THAN
YOUR EXAM RESULTS!